Performance
Appraisal

Pocket Mentor Series

The *Pocket Mentor* Series offers immediate solutions to common challenges managers face on the job every day. Each book in the series is packed with handy tools, self-tests, and real-life examples to help you identify your strengths and weaknesses and hone critical skills. Whether you're at your desk, in a meeting, or on the road, these portable guides enable you to tackle the daily demands of your work with greater speed, savvy, and effectiveness.

Books in the series:

Performance Appraisal

Expert Solutions to
Everyday Challenges

Harvard Business Press

Boston, Massachusetts

ISBN13: 978-1-4221-2883-1

The paper used in this publication meets the requirements of the American National
Standard for Permanence of Paper for Publications and Documents in Libraries and
Archives Z39.48-1992.

Contents

Test Yourself   59

A helpful review of concepts presented in this guide. Take it before and after you've read the guide, to see how much you've learned.

Answers to test questions   62

To Learn More   65

Further titles of articles and books if you want to go more deeply into the topic.

Sources for Performance Appraisal   73

Notes   75

For you to use as ideas come to mind.

Mentor's Message: Why Appraise Performance?

As a manager, you need to regularly appraise your employees' job performance. By doing so, you can reinforce stellar performance as well as help your direct reports improve subpar performance. And that generates important value for your organization, in the form of higher productivity and more positive morale throughout your team.

But appraising performance isn't easy. Many managers, for example, find it difficult to deliver constructive feedback to an employee whose performance is less than satisfactory. This book helps you master the art of performance appraisal—from preparing for an appraisal meeting and conducting the conversation to recording what happened and following up.

Kathleen Jordan, Mentor

Kathleen Jordan, PhD, is a leadership coach and organization development consultant who has worked extensively with large organizations in telecommunications, financial services, health care, and government. Her clients include AT&T, US West, Mitel Corporation, the Naval Undersea Warfare Center, and the University of Washington Medical Center. She has written articles for such publications as *Harvard Management Update*, *Harvard Business Review*, and *Design Management Journal*. Kathleen is also the collaborating writer, with authors Doug Lennick and Fred Kiel, PhD, for *Moral Intelligence: The Key to Leadership Effectiveness and Business Performance* (Financial Times Prentice Hall, 2005).

Performance Appraisal: The Basics

An Overview of Performance Appraisal

APPRAISING YOUR employees' performance is a big part of being a manager. But what does it mean, exactly? Why is it important? And what role do employees play in the appraisal process? We explore all these questions below.

What is performance appraisal?

Performance appraisal is the process you use to evaluate and support your employees' on-the-job performance. It is part of a system of performance management that is based on goals you and your employees set together. It includes the periodic informal reviews you use to see how well your employees are performing relative to their goals and to provide opportunities for early intervention.

It also includes formal performance appraisals, which are conducted at least once a year. They help you and your employees focus on the formal goals and performance expectations that can affect workers' pay, merit increases, or promotions. Appraisal sessions are both a confirmation and a formalization of the ongoing feedback that should be part of every manager's relationship with his or her employees. As such, performance appraisals should never contain any surprises.

> **Tip:** Minimize surprises during the appraisal meeting by giving feedback on a regular basis. Don't keep people in the dark until the annual review rolls around.

Why is it important?

Performance appraisals are an important tool in managing your direct reports' performance. They help you gain insight into how your employees are doing in their jobs. They are also important for these reasons:

- They enable you to communicate challenging yet realistic goals to your direct reports, so employees can achieve these goals.

- They can increase productivity by providing timely feedback to employees.

- They help your organization make decisions about workers' pay, professional development, and promotions.

- They provide protection against legal suits by employees who have been terminated, demoted, or denied a merit increase.

What role do your employees play?

Performance appraisals are an opportunity for you and each of your employees to sit down together to work on goals and challenges. As a manager, think of the review process as a partnership with your direct report. It is important to involve your employee in every stage of the appraisal process, so that you can see both sides of the story. This includes having your employee complete a self-appraisal.

"The skill to do comes from the doing."
—Cicero

In the self-appraisal, the employee evaluates his or her own performance against the goals defined for the appraisal period. The person also often identifies factors that hindered or supported performance. For example, perhaps failure to receive adequate training prevented the individual from meeting a new goal. Or maybe collaboration with team members enabled him or her to achieve an important objective.

The person may summarize his or her achievements ("I completed an important project on time, within budget, and to quality standards," "I closed five new accounts") and cite resources needed for past and future development (for example, training, new job assignments, or better equipment).

The self-appraisal format can vary from a formal, written report to an informal "jot down some notes" record. "Sample Self-Appraisal" shows an excerpt from the informal self-appraisal that one employee, a customer service representative, prepared.

Sample Self-Appraisal

Goals for appraisal period (√ for goals accomplished; X for goals not accomplished):

- √ Reduce by 10 percent the number of calls needed to solve customers' problems.
- X Learn to use new customer database.
- √ Improve knowledge of new product lines.

I wasn't able to learn the new customer database, because the workshop was postponed. Would like to try to reschedule for sometime in the coming quarter. The other goals worked out great, because my mentor was able to spend time with me explaining the new phone script and product lines.

Goals I'd like to achieve during the next period:

- Get familiar with the new customer database.
- Serve as a mentor to new hires.
- Learn more about how to deal with really difficult customers.

What I like and don't like most about my job:

I love working with the team and having a chance to try new things! The challenge for me is being confronted with an angry customer. I get very nervous and forget what I'm supposed to say.

If there's a class or workshop on dealing with difficult customers that I could take in the next few months, that would help me.

The important thing is to get the employee's perspective on his or her own job performance. Involving the person in the process is also beneficial for the following reasons:

- It sets the tone of partnership for all reviews, both formal and informal.

- It reduces any negative reactions to feedback you give the person.

- It promotes a trusting relationship between you and your employee.

Tip: Ask direct reports to rate their own performance using copies of the appraisal form you'll use in the meeting.

Preparing for a Performance Appraisal Meeting

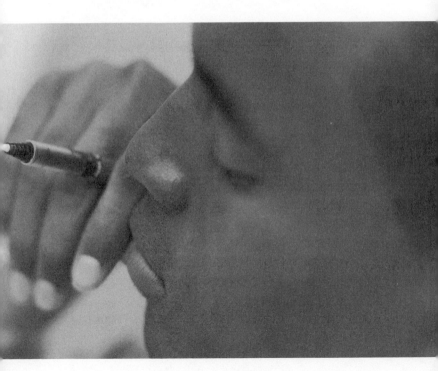

Like any other kind of meeting, a performance appraisal meeting is more productive if you're well prepared for it. Preparation includes compiling a comprehensive picture of your employee's on-the-job performance, evaluating the person's performance, documenting your impressions, and gathering the right materials. We discuss each of these tasks below.

Forming a complete picture

Evaluating your employee's performance requires reviewing multiple sources of information so you can form as complete a picture as possible of the employee's performance. These sources of information include the following:

- The requirements of the job, as stated in the job description

- The employee's own performance goals—for example, "learning to give effective presentations," "making fewer errors in processing customer orders," or "trying my hand at leading a team"

- Your criteria for successful performance

- The employee's job history, including skills, past training, and past job performance

- Your own documentation of performance observations and other relevant data

- Self-reporting by the employee

- If possible, 360-degree feedback—impressions from the full circle of people who interact with the individual, which could include customers, peers, and the employee's own direct reports, in addition to your own impressions

You may need to improvise on some of these items. For example, what if your employee does not have a current job description? In this case, use goals and other documentation that you have agreed to in the absence of a more formal job description. You or a human resource manager should then write a current job description to bring to the performance appraisal meeting, so that you can use that as a baseline from then on.

Also, if you decide to gather 360-degree feedback on your employees, apply the following practices to ensure that you get the most useful information:

- **Base feedback on crystal-clear criteria.** For example, if you're gathering input on hard-to-measure qualities such as "communication ability" or "integrity," don't just ask respondents to rate the employee on a numerical scale. Also ask for specific examples of what respondents mean by these qualities. For instance, "Joe always does what he says he's going to do. That's why I gave him a five for integrity." Balance hard-to-quantify qualities with easily quantifiable ones, such as sales figures or error rates.

- **Clarify the tool's purpose.** Explain to respondents and employees that the purpose of the 360 is to help define areas for improvement—not to amass negative feedback and "dump"

What Would YOU Do?

Sounding the Wrong Note?

D OUG IS A NEW manager in a division at Sharper Edge, a large strategy consultancy. He supervises a team of consultants, and has just begun conducting a performance appraisal meeting with Alexa, one of his direct reports. He starts out by complimenting Alexa on her outstanding client management skills: "Our best clients are singing your praises," he says. Then Doug gives Alexa some positive feedback on her ability to stay within budget and meet deadlines. "You've really hit the right notes on these aspects of your job," he tells her. Alexa grins.

Seeing her response, Doug decides that he can comfortably move on to a more problematic area—the poor execution of Alexa's monthly reports on long-term client projects that the company is working on. He explains that the reports are important documents used by consultants throughout the company to share best practices and learn from one another's experiences. Alexa seems surprised. She says that if she had known how important the reports were, she would have spent more time on them. As the meeting ends, Doug senses that Alexa feels unfairly criticized. He wonders why and what he should do differently.

What would YOU do? The mentors will suggest a solution in *What You COULD Do.*

it on employees. Remind respondents (whether they're peers, direct reports, or customers of the employee in question) that if they have concerns about their working relationship with the employee, they should address those concerns directly with the individual—not use the 360 to avoid potentially painful confrontations.

- **Build a culture of trust.** Successful use of 360-degree feedback hinges on a foundation of trust. You can build that foundation by having employees nominate their reviewers, and by allowing reviewers to remain anonymous if they wish. Also try to obtain feedback from several types of respondents for each employee. For example, ask several peers, direct reports, and customers to provide input, not just one person from each of those categories. That way, the recipient of the feedback will know that you've gathered a balanced set of data.

Tip: Make information gathering ongoing. Don't wait until the week of the appraisal meeting to gather important information about the employee.

Evaluating the employee's performance

Once you've gathered information from the many different sources described above, sit down with it and sift through it to begin forming impressions. As you do this, give equal time to good performance as well as to problems. Search for specific examples that can be supported with documentation and that are worthy of discussion during the upcoming performance appraisal meeting. For example, perhaps there's been a measurable increase in the number of new accounts closed by your employee. There are also testimonials from customers or clients citing specific talents they appreciate about the person—such as his or her ability to understand customers' problems and solve them quickly and permanently.

Some companies require managers to come up with a general rating of the employee's performance or to express different aspects of performance using a rating system or a combination of ratings and more qualitative information. Before preparing your notes about your employee's performance, refer to your company's guidelines so you can be sure you're presenting your evaluation in the required format.

"Turn appraisal into genuine opportunities for praising, for saying what's good ... which is something that most of us don't do enough of."
—Ann Limb, former group chief executive, Ufi

For good or superior performance, make sure you know what specific details support the claim. The more specific the feedback, the more likely the employee can repeat and even improve on those behaviors. For instance, suppose Sarah, a direct report, learns that her ability to listen empathetically to customers' problems has helped her generate more sales than others on her team. By understanding the power of this skill, she can strive to use it even more on the job—and even help team members master the art of empathetic listening.

For performance that needs improvement, try to identify the causes behind the less-than-ideal performance. Did the employee misunderstand expectations or instructions? Did he or she lack the required knowledge or skill to carry out the job? Was the person confused about priorities, and channeling time and effort into the wrong priorities?

Don't forget to ask yourself how you may have contributed to or interfered with your employee's performance. Consider some of the following factors that could be a supervisory responsibility:

- You may not have articulated your expectations or given the employee clear direction.

- You may not have provided the person with adequate assistance and resources.

- You may not have given the direct report training or job assignments that enabled him or her to acquire the knowledge or skills needed to do the job.

- You may have failed to use the right approaches to motivating the person to excel in his or her role.

- You may have inadvertently eroded the employee's self-confidence—for example, by failing to praise good performance often enough or by delivering overly harsh criticism.

Some poor performance on the part of employees can be attributed to what's called the *set-up-to-fail syndrome*. This syndrome is so prevalent that it merits a closer look here. Indeed, Jean-Francois Manzoni and Jean-Louis Barsoux wrote about it in the March 1998 issue of *Harvard Business Review*. Here's what they have to say about the syndrome:

> *You start with a positive relationship. Then something—a missed deadline, a lost client—makes you question the employee's performance. You begin micromanaging him. Suspecting your reduced confidence, the employee starts doubting himself. He stops giving his best, responds mechanically to your controls, and avoids decisions. You view his new behavior as additional proof of mediocrity—and tighten the screws further.*
>
> *Why not just fire him? Because you're likely to repeat the pattern with others. Better to reverse the dynamic instead. Unwinding the set-up-to-fail spiral actually pays big dividends: your company gets the best from your employees—and from you.*

If you suspect that you may have triggered a set-up-to-fail cycle with a particular employee, how do you reverse it? Consider these suggestions from Manzoni and Barsoux:

1. Choose a neutral, nonthreatening location; use affirming language ("Let's discuss our relationship and roles"); and acknowledge your part in the tension.

2. Agree on the employee's weaknesses and strengths. Support assessments with facts, not feelings.

3. Unearth causes of the weaknesses. Do you disagree on priorities? Does your employee lack specific knowledge or skills? Ask, "How is my behavior making things worse for you?"

4. Identify ways to boost performance. Training? New experiences? Decide the quantity and type of supervision you'll provide. Affirm your desire to improve matters.

5. Agree to communicate more openly: "Next time I do something that communicates low expectations, can you let me know immediately?"

If you *haven't* triggered a set-up-to-fail cycle but want to practice preventive measures, here are additional suggestions from Manzoni and Barsoux:

- Establish expectations with new employees early. Loosen the reins as they master their jobs.

- Regularly challenge your own assumptions. Ask, "What are the *facts* regarding this employee's performance?" "Is he really that bad?"

- Convey openness, letting employees challenge your opinions. They'll feel comfortable discussing their performance and relationship with you.

Documenting your impressions

It is important to record your observations and impressions about your employee's job performance as factually as possible. There are special legal considerations when documenting employee performance, so consult your human resource manager or internal legal team. If you don't have such a resource in your organization, you could consult a lawyer who specializes in employment law. This is especially advisable when an employee's performance is beginning to suffer or if you believe you may need to fire the person for his or her poor performance.

When documenting specific examples of positive *or* negative employee performance, include the following information:

- Date of the incident

- What you observed—for example, "Tina helped Jeff learn how to use the new customer database"

- Supporting data (such as reports or other people's feedback)

- Impact of the performance on your team and organization—for instance, "After Jeff learned the new database, our team began fulfilling orders more quickly, which improved cash flow for the organization"

Do not trust your memory; write your observations and impressions down. But keep the tone in your documents neutral. That is, express as much of it as possible in the form of facts ("Mark processed 10 percent of his customers' orders late") rather than judgments ("Mark doesn't know how to process orders").

And don't include anything that you would not be comfortable testifying to in a witness chair. Be especially careful to avoid using personal characterizations, such as "Jim doesn't seem to care about the team."

Gathering the right materials

To support your conversation with your employee during the performance appraisal meeting, you need to gather the following documents to bring to the meeting:

- Completed performance appraisal form that you've filled out in your company's required format

- Copy of the job description for the employee you'll be meeting with

- Employee's goals for the appraisal period

- Any documentation that supports your appraisal—such as customer testimonials, 360-degree evaluations, or objective reports related to your employee's performance (such as sales records or production reports)

Steps for Preparing for a Performance Appraisal Meeting

1. **Schedule early.** Notify the employee of the meeting well in advance. This gives both you and your direct report plenty of time to prepare for the meeting. Pick a time (for example, *not* during a lunch hour) and place (a quiet conference room) that will minimize distractions.

2. **Agree on content.** Discuss the nature of the meeting with the employee. Give the employee a copy of your company's appraisal form,

and ask him or her to complete a self-appraisal. Agree on what will be discussed during the meeting (for example, the self-appraisal, a review of your completed appraisal form, a summary of the person's strengths and areas for improvement, and the creation of a development plan).

3. **Agree on process.** Agree on the process and sequence of the meeting. For example, specify how much time will be spent on discussion, problem solving, and action planning. Establish ground rules for communication (such as "no interrupting" or "two-way feedback") to ensure constructive feedback and careful listening.

4. **Choose a neutral location.** If possible, meet in neutral territory, such as a conference room, rather than in your office. This helps establish open communication between you and your employee. Select a room that allows you and the employee to sit at the same desk or table. (If you sit behind a desk while the employee sits on a chair in front of the desk, you'll convey dominance, which won't help you cultivate the spirit of partnership you need to conduct an effective performance appraisal.)

What You COULD Do.

Remember Doug's concern about the performance appraisal meeting with Alexa?

Here's what the mentor suggests:

In preparation for the performance appraisal meeting, Doug might have considered why there was a problem with Alexa's monthly reports and how he might have contributed to the problem. For example, had he failed to provide Alexa with clear direction or to set appropriate expectations regarding the reports? Did he not explain the purpose of the reports (knowledge and best-practice sharing throughout the firm) to her?

During the meeting, Doug might have offered to help Alexa on her next batch of monthly reports to show her how they could be improved. Or he could have provided the explanatory information about the reports to her, so she could understand why he cared so much about them.

Finally, as the meeting drew to a close, Doug might have asked Alexa for *her* suggestions on ways to do things differently in the future. For instance, if Alexa often failed to submit reports on time because she was overwhelmed with other administrative tasks, she might suggest that the team hire a part-time administrative assistant to handle some of the workload. That way, consultants would be freed up to focus on their client work and the monthly reports that are so important.

Conducting the Appraisal Meeting

Y OU'VE PREPARED FOR the performance appraisal meeting you'll be holding with your employee. Now how do you conduct the actual meeting? Below are some suggestions, including how to set the right tone at the outset, how to discuss performance and address a performance problem, and how to provide useful feedback to help your direct report continue delivering good performance or improve subpar performance.

Setting the right tone

Many employees (as well as managers!) feel anxious when approaching performance appraisal meetings. From an employee's perspective, it's not easy knowing that you may be hearing some constructive criticism from your manager. (Think about times when, as an individual contributor or a manager, you've been anticipating being reviewed by your own boss.) And from the manager's perspective, it's awkward knowing that you may need to criticize a direct report and that he or she may become defensive or upset. In fact, it's fair to say that many people downright dread performance appraisals.

To mitigate any anxiety on either of your parts, it's vital that you set a tone of partnership right from the beginning. Start the meeting by reviewing the purpose and objectives of the performance appraisal: "We're going to go over what you've accomplished over the past six months and address any issues." Note the benefits of the meeting for both parties: "This meeting will help us determine how you can meet your goals. And it'll help me understand more about what you need to excel in your job." This approach prepares you and the employee for the rest of the meeting and acts as a warm-up for open dialogue.

You can further ease any nervousness on your part by remembering that a performance appraisal meeting is not meant to be a confrontational or unpleasant event. Rather, the purpose of the appraisal is to help support your employee and to promote excellent performance. To stay focused, bring clear agenda notes and use the opening of the meeting as an opportunity to establish rapport with your employee.

After reviewing the purpose and objectives of the meeting, ask the employee to talk about the self-appraisal that he or she completed beforehand. This helps you begin understanding the person's perspective on his or her performance. It also prevents you from controlling too much of the conversation early on—which can intimidate employees and keep them from sharing information openly.

As the person talks, listen carefully, and don't interrupt until your direct report has had his or her say. Demonstrate that you are listening by repeating what you've heard. For example, "If I understand you correctly, you feel that you are meeting all goals with respect to the weekly sales reports, but that you are struggling to contact all the key customers you've been assigned. Do I have that right?" By paraphrasing in this way, you give the person the opportunity to correct any misperceptions or expand on his or her points to further clarify things.

Discussing the employee's performance

As we've seen, the purpose of a performance appraisal meeting is to acknowledge and encourage good performance as well as to identify and correct any poor performance. In both cases, you need to base the conversation on specific business outcomes compared to agreed-upon performance goals. For example, "We agreed that you would increase your sales by five percent this quarter, and you exceeded that goal—you increased your sales by seven percent" or "We agreed that you'd reduce the number of production-line errors by ten percent over the past six months, but the number of errors has stayed the same as during the preceding period."

Keep the focus on the performance, and make sure not to personalize it by saying anything that could be perceived as a statement about the employee's character or values (such as "You don't seem to be really committed to these goals").

"Nothing is more terrible than activity without insight."
—Thomas Carlyle

This is also a time to confirm that the employee understands what his or her responsibilities are and that he or she has the requisite skills and resources. You'll also want to talk about any coaching and training that might be required for the person to improve his or her skills, motivation, or confidence.

Finally, you'll need to outline next steps. Spell out the specific actions you, the employee, or others will take and when. For positive performance, consider what actions can help sustain or strengthen the performance. To illustrate, "You'll continue exercising good listening skills with customers and try using this skill with new accounts." For poor performance, identify actions that can help lead to improvement. For example, "Once a week for the next two months, you'll sit in on phone calls between Sally and customers, so you can observe how she listens to them and solves their problems."

Seek agreement on and commitment to these next steps from the employee. Toward the end of the meeting, establish the time and goals for your next follow-up meeting. For instance, "Let's meet again in two weeks for an hour to go over the plan as it's been implemented so far, and to address any difficulties or surprises."

Tip: Don't let the performance appraisal form dictate the interview. Doing so can lock you and the employee into an item-by-item negotiation of specific issues and make the employee defensive.

What Would YOU Do?

Just Short of the Goal Line

C LAUDE IS EVALUATING Ricka's performance. She has had a solid record in the past. Last year, Claude and Ricka agreed on ambitious goals, with the objective that Ricka would move into the top tier of the group's performance standards. As he reviews Ricka's performance, Claude sees that although her performance has improved, she has not quite met the goal of moving into the top tier.

Claude thinks about the circumstances during the past year that prevented Ricka from meeting her goal. His top performer was promoted and left the team. That person was replaced by a new employee who is not yet up to speed. Ricka has spent much of her time helping the new person learn the ropes. Claude ponders how he should address Ricka's performance record when he meets with her.

Should he recognize that Ricka has not met her stated, measurable objectives—and discuss how to close this performance gap? Should he recognize Ricka's improvement and, given the circumstances, say that he feels she's met the objective? Should he acknowledge the role he played in Ricka's inability to meet the stated objective? Claude's head is starting to spin.

What would YOU do? The mentors will suggest a solution in *What You COULD Do.*

Addressing a performance problem

Giving an employee feedback to correct poor performance may seem difficult or uncomfortable to you. After all, no one likes to receive criticism, right? And what if your direct report becomes defensive or upset? What will you do? However, feedback to address a performance problem is critical to managing your direct reports. Without it, your employees won't know that there's a problem—and they won't be able to correct it. That can hurt your entire team's performance as well as your career.

To ease any discomfort you may feel about providing critical feedback, remember that you are working together with your employee as a team and that feedback is a necessary part of improving performance.

Begin discussing a performance problem by describing the gap between the goal and actual performance: "We were aiming for ten new accounts by the end of the quarter, and we closed seven." If possible, identify an organizational objective that explains why the problem must be resolved. For example, "The company really needs to increase sales of new products so we can build market share in the face of new competition. So each of us needs to do our part toward raising the percentage of sales of new offerings to sales of existing offerings. That's why it's important that you meet the goal we've established."

Also point out how improving performance in specific ways matters in terms of the individual's career goals. For instance, "Meeting these sales targets will position you to be eligible for a promotion and a salary increase next year." People can and do change when they understand the consequences of their behaviors and work.

Make sure the employee affirms your statements and agrees on the importance of improving his or her performance. Then move the discussion toward identifying the root cause of substandard performance. Ask the person why he or she may not be achieving desired goals. Listen carefully for the response. If you don't receive a thoughtful reply, probe with other questions. For example, "Could the problem be that you need more training?" or "Are there too many distractions in the office?"

Remember, you'll get the best results addressing performance problems if you are firm but nonthreatening. There may be many legitimate reasons for performance problems. For example, sometimes a person's performance can suffer if he or she is having family or other personal problems. However, in this case, while you can be sympathetic, you must still discuss the issues with him or her honestly and openly. Explain that you understand the person has been under a lot of pressure. Then review job expectations to ensure that they're clear. Discuss possible solutions together (for example, obtaining part-time help or counseling), and help the person to prioritize his or her work (by identifying which projects or tasks are most important). Through these means, you give your direct report the best possible chances of reaching the agreed-upon goals.

Clarity, firmness, and honesty are vital for performance appraisal at any level in an organization. Amelia Fawcett, a vice chairman at Morgan Stanley International, described her experience with and views on the subject as follows:

> *We pulled [the employee] in and told him in a very straightforward, honest, direct, aggressive but constructive way, why he was behaving in a way that was contrary to*

the culture and the interests of the firm. He had six weeks to show significant progress, and, frankly, if he didn't make significant progress we would ask him to leave. It was a very uncomfortable meeting for all three of us, but I'm delighted to say that he took the criticism on board, he worked on it immediately and became very much a team player. He has gone on to be successively promoted.

The question for all of us is often . . . wouldn't it be easier to sugar-coat the message? The lesson for me is that the soft option is never an option. It's not fair to the individual concerned; it's not fair to the firm and its clients.

Offering useful feedback

Identifying the root cause of gaps between desired and actual performance will, in most cases, create an atmosphere of objectivity in which both you and your direct report can contribute in positive ways. Your statements won't seem like attacks to your direct report; consequently, he or she will be less likely to go on the defensive. Instead, you'll be working together to address "the issue," which can often be something external to the employee—such as a lack of proper training, too few resources (or the wrong resources), or a disruptive workplace environment.

FEEDBACK *n* **1:** evaluative or corrective information transmitted to the original or controlling source about an action, event, or process

---

of the following strategies may help you offer useful feed-
an employee who needs to improve some aspect of his or
her job performance:

- Have the employee articulate any points of disagreement he
  or she has with you regarding the performance in question.
  Points of disagreement (for example, "I thought you wanted
  me to increase sales by three percent") may reveal the exis-
  tence of unclear expectations or direction.

- Orient feedback toward problem solving and action, and
  away from blame or judgment. To keep the ownership of the
  problem with the employee, give the employee the first opportunity to suggest a plan for eliminating the performance
  gap. He or she may have good ideas!

- Give feedback without the use of subjective, general attrib-
  utes. Comments such as "You aren't a leader" or "You aren't
  committed" are not helpful.

- Avoid generalizations, such as "You just don't seem involved
  with your work," in favor of specific comments that relate to
  the job. For example, "I have noticed that you haven't offered
  any suggestions at our service improvement meetings. Why
  is that?"

- Be selective in the data you choose to share. You don't need
  to recite every shortcoming or failing you've noticed while
  considering the employee's performance. Stick to the problems that *really* matter. That way, you won't make the person
  feel overwhelmed by information or devastated because

you're dumping a huge load of negative news on him o
all at once.

- Give authentic praise as well as meaningful criticism. Even an employee who's drastically underperforming in one or more areas will almost certainly be doing some things well. Acknowledge those accomplishments and abilities. You'll make it far easier for the person to hear and absorb any critical feedback you need to convey. Remember times in your own life when someone else focused only on what you were doing wrong. Then make sure you don't inflict that kind of pain on your employee.

Steps for Conducting a Performance Appraisal Meeting

1. **Set the stage.** Be welcoming when the employee comes in. Try to make the employee feel as comfortable as possible. Also review the agreed-upon content for the meeting. This helps prepare both of you and serves as a "warm-up" for open dialogue. Review guidelines, such as working together as partners on performance issues. Remind the employee that his or her input is necessary and valuable.

2. **Let the employee start the discussion.** Have the employee discuss his or her own appraisal first. Avoid trying to control the conversation. Ask probing questions to uncover the employee's perspective and assessment. For example, "How do you feel things

are going on the job?" "What's going well and what problems are you having?" Work to understand the employee's point of view. This is the time to focus on his or her understanding, not the time to agree or disagree with what you're hearing.

3. **Give and receive feedback.** Make appraisal a two-way process. Let the individual know how you view his or her performance against agreed-upon goals. State points of agreement and then compare opinions. For example, say, "Let me summarize how I see your performance, then we can compare our perceptions."

   Reinforce what the individual has done well. For instance, tell the employee, "You've done a terrific job in organizing the quarterly sales meetings, and your contributions at staff meetings are exemplary. Keep it up!"

   Also summarize where improvement is needed. For example, "So, as it stands, you need to increase your weekly customer contacts." Avoid generalizations such as, "You just don't seem motivated," in favor of specific comments that relate to the job. For example, "I've noticed that you've missed several consecutive deadlines. What's behind that?"

   Seek shared understanding of the need for improvement. To illustrate, "Could you summarize what you heard regarding the need for improvement?" Wait for a response. Encourage the employee to respond to points of disagreement, asking for clarification if necessary: "I'm not sure what you mean by that. Give me an example."

4. **Develop and agree on a development plan (or do this as a follow-up item if preferred).** Avoid a climate of "blaming"; emphasize problem solving instead: "Over the next six months, how

can we eliminate the performance issues we've discussed?" Let the employee suggest a plan for improving performance in problem areas: "How would you go about working on this?"

React to and perhaps expand on the employee's ideas in the development plan. This will make him or her less defensive. If he or she cannot formulate a good development plan, or seems unmotivated to do so, take a more direct approach. Include task assignments, training programs, experimentation with new approaches, working closely with a more skilled associate, or a change in goals.

Identify specific ways in which you can better support the employee and provide resources that will help to improve performance. Seek the employee's agreement. Communicate the consequences for improving or not improving: "I'd like to be able to consider you for a promotion when you've made progress in this area." "This is an essential requirement for someone in this job. I'm optimistic that you'll make progress."

5. **Wrap up.** Summarize feedback, beginning with positive comments first. Confirm next steps for improving performance, where applicable. Review new performance goals and the development plan to achieve them. Before concluding the meeting, conduct a brief review. Ask the employee what was useful and not so useful about the meeting. Also ask for suggestions about what you could do to make future feedback sessions more helpful. For instance, perhaps you could provide more specific examples of what you mean by good or poor performance. Or maybe you could allow more time for discussion. Thank the employee for his or her commitment.

What Would YOU Do?

Remember Claude's uncertainty about how to address Ricka's performance shortfall?

Here's what the mentor suggests:

Ricka has improved, and recognizing her improvement is a good way to start the meeting. Although Ricka has not met her stated objective, changing circumstances made that goal less realistic and achievable. Claude should acknowledge those circumstances, as well as his role in not revisiting and revising the goal in light of the changes.

During the year, Claude should have revisited Ricka's goals with her and revised them to reflect the group's changing circumstances. When he set this stretch goal with Ricka, it may have been achievable and realistic. However, during the year, it became less realistic, and perhaps not even achievable.

While Claude wants to acknowledge his role in not revisiting the goal, he should also ask Ricka to help identify goals that might need revisiting in the future. Periodic informal reviews throughout the year can help him revise goals that are no longer realistic, as well as identify and intervene if there are any performance problems.

Recording the
Meeting

RECORDING WHAT YOU and your employee discuss and decide during the performance appraisal meeting can help you both track progress and stay focused on the agreed-upon goals. Recording can take two forms: notes that you take during or after the meeting, and a development plan that you and the employee create to guide performance improvement. Below are ideas for handling each of these recording tasks.

Taking notes

If you want to take notes during the meeting, state this desire up front and identify the purpose of the note taking. For example, "Is it okay with you if I take some notes to document what we're discussing, so we can both remember what we've agreed to and keep track of our next steps?" If note taking makes you or the employee uncomfortable, it's probably better just to summarize the meeting afterward in a set of brief notes. Include in your notes or summary:

- The date of the meeting

- Who attended (in some performance appraisal meetings, your own boss or a person from the human resource department may attend, in addition to yourself and the employee)

- Key points and phrases the employee used (not necessarily verbatim), including things he or she said while presenting his or her self-appraisal

- Key points and phrases you used during the meeting

- Any points of disagreement between you and the employee on matters such as performance shortfalls or expectations

- An overview of any development plan you and your direct report discussed

- Agreed-upon next steps

"Sample Meeting Notes" shows how one manager summarized what happened during a performance appraisal meeting with her employee.

Sample Meeting Notes

Date: February 10, 2009

Attendees: Janice Molloy, marketing manager; Clark Davis, copywriter

Notes:

- Clark says he's excited about all the new clients we're taking on.
- Feels good about the "edgier" tone we're experimenting with in our copy.
- Is having trouble meeting accelerated deadlines from our biggest clients.

- Told him he had nailed the new approach on most printed pieces but was off-brand on the Goltz Enterprises and the GenArc accounts.
- He agreed on the Goltz and GenArc; said he hadn't taken enough time to review the raw materials before drafting the copy. Felt bad about "wasting our time and theirs."
- Next steps: he'll commit to taking sufficient time for project review before jumping in. Re missing deadlines: he'll hire freelancers to take on easier copy-writing jobs in the next six months.

Creating a development plan

A development plan is an important tool for addressing improvements in skills or behaviors that you and the employee have decided should be worked on in the future. If you have prepared a draft of this document in advance of the meeting, and if time permits, you can discuss it toward the end of an appraisal session. Often both parties need more time or additional information and prefer to reconvene to develop the plan together as a follow-up item after the meeting.

DEVELOPMENT PLAN *n* **1:** a document specifying how an employee will reach expected performance outcomes

In either case, you and your employee need to work together to reach agreement on a development plan. You must then seek commitment from your employee to achieve the goals of the plan. A thorough development plan includes:

- Timeline
- Action steps
- Expected outcomes
- Training required, if applicable
- Specific goals
- Feedback required
- Practice required

The development plan then becomes part of the employee's record. "Geena's Development Plan" shows a simplified example of how such a plan might look.

Geena's Development Plan

Timeline: by end of month
Action steps: Geena takes one-day course on using the new customer database
Expected outcomes: Geena takes test and gets passing grade
Goals: Geena begins using new database by middle of next month
Feedback required: outcomes on order-fulfillment cycle time and on data-entry errors made while using the database
Practice required: spend two hours per week observing two team members using new database

"Make a Development Plan" provides an opportunity for you to try your hand at this important task.

Make a Development Plan

You've recently met with several employees to discuss their job performance. Now try your hand at crafting a development plan for them.

Part 1: Managing Carl

The conversation with Carl went well, with plenty of positive discussion. After the meeting, you jot down the following notes:

- Gives a lot of credit to his team members.
- Said company "takes care of me," provides him with "excellent motivation to go above and beyond."
- He'd like to see changes in the way new projects are managed.

You realize that Carl is a high performer, and you want to create a development plan that will help him continue making important contributions. Which of the following steps would you recommend in the plan?

1. Have Carl focus on leading established projects, since he seems uncomfortable with the way new projects are managed.
2. Continue having Carl lead established and new projects. But ask him to work within the new-project management methods already developed by the group.
3. Suggest that Carl review the process that the company currently uses for handling new projects, and propose ideas for improvement.

If you picked option 3, you have a good sense of how to create a development plan. Carl expressed interest in seeing changes in the company's new-project management methods. Reviewing the existing methods and proposing improvements would help keep this high performer engaged and challenged. It could also lead to the generation of valuable new ideas for the company.

Options 1 and 2 would be less effective, because neither of them would give Carl an opportunity to grow. And growth should be the goal of a development plan for a high-performing employee.

Part 2: Managing Marla

Marla is doing very well as a programmer. During your appraisal meeting with her, you took the following notes:

- So far has worked on simpler projects, which she is able to handle with little trouble.
- Believes she's ready to take on more complex, interactive programs.
- Might do well in Hank's program, with lots of interactive elements—Marla likes the idea.

Which of the following steps would you take next to further Marla's development?

1. Invite Marla to commit to working in Hank's program.
2. Ask Hank whether he has room for Marla on his project team.
3. See whether Marla would be interested in training new employees.

If you picked option 2, you're on the right track. You need to make sure that your idea for Marla's development—taking part in Hank's program—will work out in practical terms.

Option 1 would be less effective as a next step. If you haven't explored the practical ramifications of your idea, gaining Marla's commitment could end in disappointment for her if it turns out that Hank doesn't have room for her on his project team.

Option 3 would also be less effective, because nothing during the meeting suggested that Marla has interest in training new employees. You should follow up on the new challenges in which she did express interest—which center on taking on more complex programs.

Following Up

C ONDUCTING A performance appraisal meeting is just one part of effectively managing your employee's performance. You also need to follow up after each meeting. That means monitoring the person's progress toward agreed-upon goals, as well as stepping back and assessing your own skill as a manager at appraising your direct reports' performance.

Monitoring the employee's progress

After you have completed your performance appraisal, make sure both you and the employee have a copy of the development plan or a written record of next steps and commitments.

You should plan on following up after every appraisal meeting. High performers and satisfactory performers will likely need less follow-up from you. However, if you've given them new, more demanding goals than they've had in the past, you'll want to monitor their progress and determine whether they need additional training, coaching, or support.

Employees with performance gaps who have committed to development plans should be more carefully monitored. In most cases, monitoring takes the form of a follow-up meeting every few weeks or months. Your goal in these meetings is to check on your employee's progress against his or her development plan, and to provide coaching if necessary.

Evaluating your approach

Most managers find that effectively appraising employees' performance takes practice. For that reason, it's important to evaluate your own approach periodically and to consider how you might make improvements.

For example, before you conclude each meeting, it's appropriate to conduct a brief review of what was useful in the meeting and what was not. For instance, perhaps the conference room you used was private and quiet, but you didn't allocate enough time for the discussion. Also ask your employee for suggestions for ways to do things differently in the future.

After each performance appraisal meeting, think about how you handled your side of the conversation. Ask yourself, "Did I create an open climate? Did I listen carefully to what the employee said? Was my feedback clear and specific? What worked well, and what could be improved on next time?"

Compare your view with any feedback you collected from your employee at the end of your meeting. Determine what changes you can make for future meetings with that person and for future meetings in general to make your approach to performance appraisal more effective.

What Would YOU Do?

Bottoms Up?

ARIA IS ABOUT to evaluate her direct reports. She dislikes this part of her job because she often feels uncertain about how to handle an evaluation. This year, she wants to focus on improving her appraisal skills.

She starts with Paul. Maria's group has a three-tiered set of performance standards. When Paul joined the group, midway through the year, Maria suggested that he start off with a goal of meeting the lowest tier. As she reviews Paul's performance, she sees that Paul has performed within this tier, but at the very bottom.

Maria is disappointed with Paul's performance. Upon reflection, Maria realizes that when she was just starting out, her performance was easily twice Paul's. Maria wonders how to approach this performance issue. Should she ask Paul why his performance has been unsatisfactory—at the bottom of the lowest tier? Should she tell him she's disappointed with his performance but that she wants to help him improve? What about acknowledging that he has successfully met his performance goal for the year?

What would YOU do? The mentors will suggest a solution in *What You COULD Do.*

What You COULD Do.

Remember Maria's concern about how to talk with Paul about his performance?

Here's what the mentor suggests:

Maria should acknowledge that Paul has successfully met his performance goal for the year: his performance is within the lowest tier, which is what they agreed on. Maria is evaluating Paul's performance against an objective that they both concurred on, and he has met that objective. When Maria and Paul set his goals for the coming year, Maria will likely want to establish stretch goals with him—and then give him the support he needs to reach the new objectives.

After recognizing that Paul has met his goal, Maria might then ask him what he thinks he needs to do to improve his performance. She should probe to understand Paul's perception of his performance and any barriers to improvement. At that point, she might also tell him that she wants to help him improve over the coming year. They can discuss how she can support Paul's efforts to meet the new stretch objectives. Also, when she is evaluating performance, it's important that Maria not use herself as a yardstick and reference for measurement. She has likely been promoted because of proven high performance. She should measure an employee's performance against the stated objectives that he and she agreed on, not on her own past performance record or expectations she may have set with her own boss in the past.

Tips and Tools

Tools for
Performance Appraisal

Preparation Checklist

*Complete this checklist to make sure you are properly
prepared for an appraisal meeting.*

Have You?	Yes	No
1. Scheduled the meeting?		
2. Given the employee notice and a copy of the appraisal form for a self-appraisal?		
3. Reviewed the job requirements?		
4. Reviewed the employee's performance goals as well as your criteria?		
5. Reviewed the employee's history, including skills, past training, and past job performance?		
6. Carefully looked for "gaps" between stated goals and actual performance?		
7. Identified the cause and effect links between the employee's attitudes and behavior and his or her performance?		
8. Completed the performance appraisal form?		
9. Noted specific strengths and how they can be enhanced or sustained during more challenging times or work assignments?		
10. Noted problems that need to be discussed, and listed specific examples?		

If you have answered no to any of the above questions, you might consider
delaying the meeting until you can answer yes to every question.

Evaluation Checklist

Complete this checklist after you've conducted a performance appraisal meeting to improve future meetings.

Question	Yes	No	Comments
1. Did you create an open climate?			
2. Did you and the employee start the meeting with an understanding of its purpose and process?			
3. Were you and the employee prepared?			
4. Did you listen carefully to what the employee said?			
5. Did you provide clear and specific feedback?			
6. Did you learn anything new about the employee that will help you coach him or her in the future?			
7. Did you learn anything new about yourself?			
8. Did the meeting end with mutual agreement about the employee's development plan?			
9. Did the meeting motivate the employee?			
10. Did the employee leave with a clear understanding of your assessment?			
11. Does the employee know what to do in the future to improve performance?			
12. Do you know what you'll change during the next appraisal meeting?			

Individual Development Plan

Use this form to help strengthen an employee's professional abilities by matching the individual's skills, business interests, and work values with opportunities for growth.

Developmental Goals	Measures of Achievement/ Expected Outcomes
1.	
2.	
3.	

Methods to Be Used

On-the-Job Learning

What challenging assignments should this employee work on to build skills and achieve developmental goals? List the goal number next to each item.

Goal #	Type of Assignment	Time Frame

Training/Education

What specific training, educational experiences, and performance support measures (including online learning) can be used to develop desired skills and assist in achieving the employee's goals? List the goal number next to each item.

Goal #	Type of Training/ Education/Support	When	Cost Estimate

Support Needed

What additional support is needed to achieve the employee's goals (coaching, mentoring, etc.)? How will it be provided?

Monitoring Progress

Who will provide feedback on the employee's progress, and how often? Be as specific as you can regarding who is involved and how often progress will be assessed.

Time Frame

Start date of plan:		Anticipated completion date:	

Agreement—This plan is agreed to as indicated by the signatures below.

Plan Participant	Date	Manager	Date

Supporting Documentation Summary Form

Use this form to summarize key information from supporting documentation you've gathered to inform your appraisal of a particular employee.

Employee name:	Title:
Date of appraisal meeting:	Department:

Instructions:

1. In column 1 below, list the documents you've gathered that have informed your appraisal of this employee. (Examples may include customer testimonials, 360-degree evaluations, and reports related to specific aspects of your employee's performance, such as sales records or production reports.)

2. In column 2, list the key points and examples you extracted from the documents.

An example has been provided for each column.

Column 1 Types of documents gathered	Column 2 Key points
Example: *360-degree evaluation*	*Example:* *Fellow members of Cora's project team reported that she excelled at staying positive during setbacks. Important areas of improvement they agreed on included the need for Cora to strengthen her familiarity with the new IT system.*

Test Yourself

This section offers ten multiple-choice questions to help you identify your baseline knowledge of the essentials of performance appraisal. Answers to the questions are given at the end of the test.

1. Complete this sentence: "Performance appraisals are part of a larger system of performance management that includes _____ and _____."

a. Setting goals *and* conducting periodic informal and formal reviews.

b. Developing specific short-term *and* long-term objectives.

c. Team vision *and* organizational strategies.

2. How frequently should you conduct a formal performance appraisal for each employee?

a. Every three months.

b. At least once every eighteen months (six fiscal quarters).

c. At least once a year.

3. Which of the following statements about performance goals is true?

   a. Goals must be challenging but achievable.

   b. An effective goal always includes a contribution to the individual's personal and career growth.

   c. Goals ideally reflect the outcome to strive for, but do not have to be fully achievable.

4. You are the manager of a customer service team. Which of the following should you *not* include in a performance review for one of your direct reports?

   a. The employee's own opinions of how he or she is doing on the job.

   b. Your opinions about what others think of his or her performance.

   c. Examples of the employee's customer service supported by documentation.

5. When you are scheduling a performance appraisal, which of these locations is suggested as the optimal setting?

   a. Off-site in a neutral setting, such as a restaurant.

   b. On-site in a business setting.

   c. On-site in the employee's office.

6. When preparing for a performance appraisal meeting, you should gather a completed appraisal form that you have filled out, a copy of the goals for the appraisal period, and the employee's completed performance appraisal form (if available). What other key document would be useful?

a. A copy of the person's job description.

b. A copy of the organization's strategy.

c. A copy of the employee's previous appraisal.

7. A suggested source of information to consider when preparing for an appraisal meeting is 360-degree feedback. What does the term *360-degree feedback* encompass?

a. Direct observation feedback from peers.

b. Feedback that includes self-reporting by the employee.

c . Feedback from customers, peers, and, if applicable, the employee's direct reports.

8. At what point during the performance appraisal meeting should the employee talk about his or her self-appraisal?

a. After you have given your performance appraisal and feedback.

b. After the initial review of the appraisal's purpose and objectives and before your feedback.

c. Before or after your performance feedback; ask the employee which would be more comfortable for him or her.

9. In discussing a performance problem, one suggested approach is to identify a "performance gap." What is a performance gap?

   a. A difference between the employee's performance goal and his or her actual performance.

   b. Lack of alignment between the employee's performance and the organization's strategy.

   c. A disparity between the employee's performance and the responsibilities listed in his or her job description.

10. True or false? When conducting a performance appraisal, you shouldn't let the performance appraisal form direct the flow of the meeting.

   a. True.

   b. False.

Answers to test questions

1, a. The performance management cycle begins with goal setting by each employee and team. Periodic informal and formal reviews provide an opportunity to see how well each employee is performing relative to his or her goals.

2, c. Most managers conduct a formal performance appraisal for each employee at least once a year. This process helps the employee and the manager focus on the formal goals and performance expectations that can impact salary, merit increases, or promotions. To manage performance effectively, though, it's also important to engage in informal, ongoing performance assessments. Information gathered at informal meetings can minimize surprises at the formal annual meeting.

3, a. Goals that are challenging but *not* achievable are frustrating and therefore will not motivate employees to commit to reaching them.

4, b. Your opinions about what others think of the employee's performance won't be helpful to the direct report. If you want to include other employees' feedback on your direct report's performance, don't provide opinions (for example, "I think the other team members are frustrated by your lack of participation in meetings"). Instead, offer facts—the actual data representing others' evaluations of the employee's performance. For instance, "Two of your five teammates said they wanted you to speak up more during meetings."

5, b. Hold the performance appraisal on-site, in a neutral business setting such as a small conference room. Pick a time and place that minimizes distractions. Also, schedule the meeting in advance so that you and the employee have enough time to prepare.

6, a. In addition to ensuring that the employee's performance meets the stated goals and is consistent with the organization's strategy and direction, the appraisal meeting is an appropriate time to ensure that the employee's performance is consistent with his or her job description.

7, c. The term *360-degree feedback* refers to the full circle of people who interact with the employee whose performance you're evaluating. These individuals could include customers, peers, and, if applicable, the employee's direct reports.

8, b. The suggested timing for having the employee talk about his or her self-appraisal is after the initial review of the meeting's purpose and objectives and before you provide your feedback. This timing helps you understand the employee's point of view and prevents you from controlling the conversation early on in the meeting.

9, a. A performance gap in an appraisal setting refers to a difference between the employee's stated written goal and his or her actual performance. Once you've jointly identified a performance gap, and if the performance goal is still valid, you and the employee can begin to develop a plan to close the gap.

10, a. When conducting a performance appraisal, you should not let the performance appraisal form direct the flow of the meeting. Doing so can lock you and the employee into an item-by-item negotiation of specific issues and make the employee defensive.

To Learn More

Articles

Allen, Peter L. "Performance Appraisals with More Gain, Less Pain." *Harvard Management Communication Letter*, March 2003.

What is the responsibility that you, as a manager, hate the most? If you are thinking performance reviews, then you have much to learn from Dick Grote, the author of *The Performance Appraisal Question and Answer Book: A Survival Guide for Managers*. His recent book, reviewed in this article, may not make you look forward to the next set of performance appraisals, but it can help you manage the process more effectively—and maybe even spare you that "I'd rather be having a root canal" feeling.

Field, Anne. "Are You Rewarding Solo Performance at the Team's Expense?" *Harvard Management Update*, August 2006.

A stated commitment to teamwork is the norm at most companies today, as standard a part of corporate life as cubicles and yearly performance reviews. Yet many performance management and incentive systems are so focused on individual contributors that they inadvertently undermine the very teamwork organizations claim to support and encourage.

This article presents advice from thought leaders and practitioners on achieving the delicate balance between motivating individual contributors to shine while simultaneously shaping them to be strong ensemble players.

Kaplan, Robert S. "What to Ask the Person in the Mirror." *Harvard Business Review* OnPoint Enhanced Edition, January 2007.

As leaders rise through the ranks, they have fewer and fewer opportunities for honest and direct feedback. Therefore, it is wise to go through a self-assessment, to periodically step back from the bustle of running a business and ask some key questions of yourself. Author Robert S. Kaplan, who during his twenty-two-year career at Goldman Sachs chaired the firm's senior leadership training efforts and cochaired its partnership committee, identifies seven areas for self-reflection: vision and priorities, managing time, feedback, succession planning, evaluation and alignment, leading under pressure, and staying true to yourself. Although the questions sound simple, people are often shocked—even horrified—by their own answers. Executives are aware that they should be focusing on their most important priorities, but without stepping back to reflect, few actually know where they are allocating their time.

Harvard Business School Publishing. "Alternatives to the Annual Performance Review." *Harvard Management Update*, February 2000.

Companies can get rid of those troublesome yearly evaluations if they really want to. But it isn't an easy move to make. Managers have to change some fundamental assumptions about what really produces high performance. Companies have to work with employees differently on a variety of fronts, from feedback to compensation.

Hattersley, Michael E. "How to Get the Best Out of Performance Reviews." *Harvard Management Communication Letter*, May 1999.

Not all workers perform equally well. How do you deal with both the good and the bad effectively? The author begins with the premise that a good performance review is an ongoing process, where nothing should come as a surprise to the employee. He then provides some illustrative examples of how supervisors at different companies handle issues such as telling the truth, managing the poor performer, coping with the average performer, and recognizing excellence.

Johnson, Lauren Keller. "The Ratings Game: Retooling 360s for Better Performance." *Harvard Management Update*, January 2004.

After earning its stripes in professional development, the 360-degree feedback tool has insinuated itself into the performance appraisal processes at an increasing number of companies. But the colleague-based feedback that has made 360s such a favored tool in development can be its Achilles' heel in performance reviews: most people possess a deep ambivalence about wielding power over a peer's livelihood. Read about how people are reshaping the tool so that it not only encourages direct and honest feedback in annual reviews, but also fits the particular needs and priorities of a broad range of organizations.

Peiperl, Maury A. "Getting 360-Degree Feedback Right." *Harvard Business Review*, January–February 2001.

One component of 360-degree feedback—peer appraisal— consistently stymies managers and heightens tension. Peiperl explores the paradoxes behind this dilemma—for example, an employee's colleagues have to juggle roles as both peers and judges. The author argues that by understanding these paradoxes, managers can make this form of performance management more effective.

Books

Edwards, Mark R., and Ann J. Ewen. *360-Degree Feedback*. New York: AMACOM, 1996.

As the title suggests, this method of performance assessment takes viewpoints from all directions: those of customers, peers, supervisors, and direct reports. The authors cite effectiveness in diversity management, team-based structures, TQM, and other broad initiatives.

Harless, Joe H. *Analyzing Human Performance: Tools for Achieving Business Results*. Alexandria, VA: American Society for Training & Development, 2000.

This tool kit for human performance improvement (HPI) professionals explains how to conduct effective performance analyses. It includes self-instructional support materials that let you learn at your own pace.

Hickman, Stew. *How to Conduct a Performance Appraisal.* Info-Line Series. Alexandria, VA: American Society for Training & Development, 2001.

Does your company's performance appraisal system work well? Could it be improved? This sixteen-page booklet provides guidelines for conducting effective performance assessments. It includes a checklist of tasks essential for preparing for and conducting a performance review.

Hodges, Toni M., and Jack J. Phillips. *In Action: Measuring Learning and Performance.* Alexandria, VA: American Society for Training & Development, 1999.

This collection of sixteen case studies reveals a variety of approaches to measuring learning and job performance. It includes practical applications of evaluation techniques such as simulations, post-tests, self-assessment, and observation.

eLearning Programs

Harvard Business School Publishing. *Case in Point.* Boston: Harvard Business School Publishing, 2004.

Case in Point is a flexible set of online cases, designed to help prepare middle- and senior-level managers for a variety of leadership challenges. These short, reality-based scenarios provide sophisticated content to create a focused view into the realities of the life of a leader. Your managers will experience Aligning Strategy, Removing Implementation Barriers,

Overseeing Change, Anticipating Risk, Ethical Decisions, Building a Business Case, Cultivating Customer Loyalty, Emotional Intelligence, Developing a Global Perspective, Fostering Innovation, Defining Problems, Selecting Solutions, Managing Difficult Interactions, The Coach's Role, Delegating for Growth, Managing Creativity, Influencing Others, Managing Performance, Providing Feedback, and Retaining Talent.

Harvard Business School Publishing. *Coaching for Results*. Boston: Harvard Business School Publishing, 2000.

Understand and practice how to effectively coach others by mastering the five core skills necessary for successful coaching:

- Observing
- Questioning
- Listening
- Feedback
- Agreement

Through interactive role-playing, expert guidance, and activities for immediate application at work, this program helps you coach successfully by preparing, discussing, and following up in any situation.

Harvard Business School Publishing. *Managing Difficult Conversations*. Boston: Harvard Business School Publishing, 2001.

This program will help you understand why disagreements occur and help you build conclusions collaboratively. These productive dialogue skills will lead to a more accurate, shared understanding of the information exchanged in your daily interactions. *Managing Difficult Conversations* examines techniques for approaching and handling difficult business conversations. The program explores how mental models influence our private thinking and, thus, our behavior. It presents the Left-Hand Column exercise as a technique for unveiling and examining our internal thought process. The program also examines five unproductive thinking habits that many people fall into during difficult conversations and five productive alternative ways of thinking. By examining your own thinking habits and actively seeking more productive mind-sets, you can learn to approach difficult conversations with confidence, avoid blaming, overcome defensiveness, and make better business decisions.

Harvard Business School Publishing. *Managing Direct Reports*. Boston: Harvard Business School Publishing, 2000.

Learn the skills and concepts you need to effectively manage direct reports and be able to apply these techniques immediately to your own situation. Through interactive practice scenarios, expert guidance, on-the-job activities, and a mentoring feature, you will learn and practice how to:

- Understand direct reports' expectations
- Manage a network of relationships
- Delegate along a continuum

Pre- and postassessments and additional resources complete the workshop, preparing you for more productive direct-report relationships.

Other Information Sources

Harvard Business School Publishing. *Working Smarter: Reforming Employee Development*. Boston: Harvard Business School Publishing, 1998.

This tool kit includes a videocassette, a blueprint, and a series of worksheets to help you conduct a 360-degree review. The video shows the review process in action, as a supervisor and her manager complete review questionnaires and develop an action plan. The blueprint and worksheets help you conduct a review with your own direct reports.

Sources for Performance Appraisal

The following sources aided in development of this book:

Beer, Michael. "Conducting a Performance Appraisal Interview." *Harvard Business School Case Note*. Boston: Harvard Business School Publishing, 1997.

Gabarro, John J., and Linda A. Hill. "Managing Performance." *Harvard Business School Case Note*. Boston: Harvard Business School Publishing, 1996.

Grote, Dick. "Making the Performance Appraisal System Work." In *The Complete Guide to Performance Appraisal*. New York: AMACOM, 1996.

Harvard Business School Publishing. *Manager's Toolkit*. Boston: Harvard Business School Press, 2004.

Johnson, Lauren Keller. "The Ratings Game: Retooling 360s for Better Performance." *Harvard Management Update*, January 2004.

Manzoni, Jean-Francois, and Jean-Louis Barsoux. "The Set-Up-to-Fail Syndrome." *Harvard Business Review*, March 1998.

Notes

Notes

Notes

Notes

Notes

Notes

Notes

Notes

Notes

Notes

Notes

How to Order

Harvard Business Press publications are available worldwide from your local bookseller or online retailer.

You can also call:
1-800-668-6780

Our product consultants are available to help you 8:00 a.m.–6:00 p.m., Monday–Friday, Eastern Time. Outside the U.S. and Canada, call: 617-783-7450.

Please call about special discounts for quantities greater than ten.

You can order online at:
www.HBSPress.org